DEAR MOM AND DAD

DEAR MOM AND DAD

*What Kids of Divorce Really
Want to Say to Their Parents*

by

GILLIAN ROTHCHILD

POCKET BOOKS
New York   London   Toronto   Sydney   Tokyo   Singapore

POCKET BOOKS, a division of Simon & Schuster Inc.
1230 Avenue of the Americas, New York, NY 10020

Copyright © 1999 by Gillian Rothchild

All rights reserved, including the right to reproduce
this book or portions thereof in any form whatsoever.
For information address Pocket Books, 1230 Avenue
of the Americas, New York, NY 10020

Rothchild, Gillian
    Dear mom and dad: a book for divorced parents whose
kids want to be happy / by Gillian Rothchild.
       p.   cm.
  ISBN 0-671-02788-3
  1. Children of divorced parents—United States. 2. Divorced
parents—United States.   I. Title
HQ777.5.R68 1999
306.89—dc21   99-12399
                                        CIP

First Pocket Books trade paperback printing April 1999

10 9 8 7 6 5 4 3 2 1

POCKET and colophon are registered trademarks of
Simon & Schuster Inc.

Cover design by Tom McKeveny

Designed by Laura Lindgren

Printed in the U.S.A.

This book is dedicated to my son, who has "been there, done that," and yet still continues to strive and survive.

Life is never a perfect package. We all have our roads to travel and karma to clean and polish. May you strive to handle them with grace and humility. May you always know that anything that happens in life is ultimately for the good. You are always blessed and protected. A peaceful mind and an open heart will always guide you to your essence.

With unconditional love always,
Mom

IT'S GOD'S CHILD GIVEN IN YOUR CARE

A mother and father's first and foremost duty is the welfare of their child. You should not place your needs ahead of your child's. Everything else should come afterward. As parents, you should realize that a beautiful soul has been given into your hands for your care. Don't harm your child by placing him or her in the middle of your own conflicts. Any problems or difficulties that you are having as husband and wife should be secondary to attending to the well-being of your child. Everything you do should be conducive to fulfilling this duty. Your child needs you and as long as he or she does, you must make a commitment to work things out in your child's best interest.

You will get the necessary strength to fulfill this duty if you know your responsibility and affirm: "Yes, God has given me this opportunity. I have to do it and I'm going to do it." God placed this child in your care and God will give you enough strength to fulfill that duty. God is not a fool to put a child in weak hands.

Maybe you do not know how you will rise to this challenge. Perhaps you question your ability to make the necessary adjustments. But maybe you have not tapped into your own strength. God will never give a baby to a mother and father who cannot take care of this child. Realize that you have the strength to fulfill your responsibility. Believe in that and go ahead and work together to take care of the beautiful angel entrusted to your care. Do everything possible to help your child grow into a beautiful, spiritual child of God.

SRI SWAMI SATCHIDANANDA

DEAR MOM AND DAD

Based on my seventeen years of experience, both professional and personal, I have come to the conclusion there is a great need for a book such as *Dear Mom and Dad.* No one has taken the time to deal with the subject of children stuck in the middle of divorce in a simple, black-and-white, right-and-wrong fashion. During the trauma of divorce you are usually not able to focus on much of anything, let alone the extra needs of your children. You are focusing on the failure of your dreams and your guilt for your children. The last thing you want to do is sit down and read a complicated book. You need a quick, didactic answer to help you and your children get on with your lives as quickly and smoothly as possible during the transition. This book is such a gift. It is the "how to take care of the children while you fall apart" book. We must make life and rules as simple as possible. This is a very traumatic time for both you and your children and the way you handle it will affect your lives forever.

The book is written simply enough for a one-sitting read and then to be used for reference. This format allows you to thumb through, whenever necessary, to gain words of wisdom and reinforcement in answering your many daily questions and challenges. It is a book that will help take away the stress, guilt, and ignorance of dealing with your new life situations as quickly and simply as possible. Know that you are not expected to be perfect and will make mistakes along the way. But, if your decisions and actions with your children come from a place of love, knowledge, and understanding, they will know and respect your efforts in the many years to come. You chose to bring these precious beings into the world, now continue to choose to nurture, protect, and love them.

DEAR MOM AND DAD

Q. *How do we make our children, whether 2 or 21, feel loved, cared for, and safe when we DIVORCE?*

A. Follow the Ten Commandments for Divorced Parents and read this book because . . . you still love your children.

TEN COMMANDMENTS

for

DIVORCED PARENTS

1. Thou shalt not make derogatory statements about the other parent.

2. Thou shalt not make your child your best friend to confide in.

3. Thou shalt not use your child as a messenger service.

4. Thou shalt not deny your child's feelings or your own.

5. Thou shalt openly give your child permission to love and respect the other parent.

6. Thou shalt not change house rules to compete with the other parent.

CONSISTENCY

+

DISCIPLINE

= LOVE

7. Thou shalt not change the visitation arrangements.

8. Thou shalt never make your child feel "stuck in the middle."

9. Thou shalt never blame or indicate the divorce is due to or revolves around your child. Divorce IS A GROWN-UP MATTER.

10. Thou shalt always practice loving, positive, and consistent parenting and make your child's world a safe and special place to live.

1. There are many ways to tell me that you are separating or divorcing. Please take the time to decide on the best way, time, and place to tell me. This is a moment I will always remember.

2. When you tell me about your divorce, please tell me where I am going to live.

~~~~~~~~~~~~~

3. Explain to me how my life may change and how it will stay the same.

~~~~~~~~~~~~~

4. Tell me that you both still love me and that you are not divorcing me too.

5. Please reassure me that I will still see both of you and have a schedule planned for me before you separate.

~~~~~~~~~~~~~~~

6. I don't want to give money or checks to Mom or Dad. Put them in the mail.

7. I am not your messenger. If you have something to say to each other, write a letter or use the telephone and do it when I'm not around.

———————

8. Money and who pays for what is none of my business.

9. Money will not buy my love. Please don't compete with presents and try to impress me with material things.

~~~~~~~~~~~~~~~

10. It's not my fault you don't get along. Don't make me feel that it is.

~~~~~~~~~~~~~~~

11. Don't get together in front of me if you can't get along.

12. Don't make me settle arguments. I am not a mediator.

~~~~~~~~~~~~~~~~

13. When it's not your weekend, please don't show up at my activities. It makes me feel uncomfortable and stuck in the middle.

14. Don't compete for my love. There is and always has been room in my heart to love both of you.

~~~~~~~~~

15. Don't try to make me lose respect for the other parent. I really do need both of you.

~~~~~~~~~

16. Please remember why you chose to bring me into this world.

17. Please don't ever force me to choose between the both of you. This is an impossible task and will make me feel guilty the rest of my life.

---

18. Please don't depend on me for emotional comfort. You are the parent and I am the child.

19. Never tell me that I am your whole life and you don't know what you would do without me. That's too much responsibility for me to handle.

~~~~~~~~~~~~~~~~

20. Allow me to love both sets of relatives and friends. The more people I have to share my love with, the happier I will be.

21. I need a structured and consistent visitation schedule.

---

22. Please remember I need quality time, not quantity time, when I'm with you.

---

23. I am not an adult. Please don't expect me to understand or behave older than my age.

24. If you feel something should be paid for by the other parent, you ask for it—not me.

------~~~~~~~~~~~------

25. I want to hug and kiss both of you. Don't make me feel guilty for doing this . . . I have not chosen to divorce either one of you.

26. Please protect me from hurtful, angry relatives. I don't want to take sides.

~~~~~~~~~~

27. The more people I have to share positive time with, the more I will grow into a healthy, well-rounded human being.

28. Encourage me to speak to and confide in other adults if I need to talk to someone. I need to be able to share my feelings with other important people in my life.

29. Special occasions will come up where both of you may be invited to attend. If you both choose to come, please don't compete for my attention. If you cannot get along, sit on opposite sides of the room.

----

30. Please accept and understand my anger, confusion, mixed feelings, and fears.

31. Living in two homes can be very overwhelming. Help me when I'm tired, scared, or irritable.

---

32. I want unconditional love.

---

33. I will begin to question your intentions if you can afford to buy me more than my other parent can and feel sad for my other parent's situation.

34. I am not a reporter or spy. Don't ask me questions about each other's lives.

----

35. How much money each of you spends on me is none of my business.

36. Please don't complain to me about visitation. This is something you have to work out between yourselves.

---

37. Please protect me from your "well-meaning" friends. I don't want to hear their opinions about you.

38. Telling me that it hurts you not to see me more and that you always miss me makes me feel uncomfortable. Please tell me how happy you are to see me instead of how miserable you are not seeing me.

~~~~~~~~~~~~~~~~~

39. Please allow me to share my friends with both of you. I really like sleepovers and want to have a normal life on the weekends too.

40. Please be a responsible parent when I have lessons, school activities, or team obligations that I have to attend. Help me to be prompt and prepared.

----

41. Two homes and two families can be very confusing at any age. Please help me to adjust by making things as simple as possible.

42. I really need to have special things at both homes.

———————

43. I need to have a homework area in each home.

———————

44. Please allow me to have family pictures by my bedside. I know you may not enjoy looking at them, but I do.

45. Please allow me to have clothing at both homes, so I am not responsible for carrying things back and forth all the time. I need your help. It's too hard to keep track of so many things.

----

46. Quiet mealtimes with you are very important. Please take the time to sit and eat with me.

47. You didn't divorce me. Please remember I belong to both of you.

~~~~~~~~~

48. I need to have a bedtime, even if you do want to spend more time with me. I will get cranky if I am not properly rested.

~~~~~~~~~

49. Please try to keep the same rules at both houses.

50. I may have problems sleeping at night during these transitions. Sit with me or hold me; help me to know that I am safe in my own room and bed at your home.

~~~~~~~~~~~~

51. Please help me to take pride in both homes and respect my family responsibilities.

52. Friends' parties and invitations are very important to me. Please try your best to help me participate in my outside activities during your time.

~~~~~~~~~~~~~~~~

53. If you are having problems setting limits for me, try using some of the guidelines we use at school. I know what is expected of me there.

54. Schoolwork is very important. Please make sure you know what I am doing and be willing to help me when I need it.

---

55. Please have some of my favorite foods at your home.

---

56. Teach me to always put things back where I find them.

57. I should have my own toiletries,
    stuffed animals, toys, books,
    tapes, or CDs at each home.

    ~~~~~~~~~~~~~

58. If I don't have anything nice to
    say, teach me not to say anything
    at all.

    ~~~~~~~~~~~~~

59. Help me to trust again. Life has
    become very frightening.

60. Show me that love does conquer the evils.

~~~~~~~~~~

61. Teach me what integrity is.

~~~~~~~~~~

62. Help me to fall in love with myself.

~~~~~~~~~~

63. Don't spoil me.

64. Please don't tell me my fears and sadness are silly. They are very real to me. Reassure me.

~~~~~~~~~~~

65. You divorced each other . . . will you someday divorce me too? Help me to know that you will always be my parent and love me.

~~~~~~~~~~~

66. Perfection is too hard. Please don't expect it of yourself or me.

67. Please don't make promises you can't keep. I am learning to trust my new life, so please help to reinforce it.

---

68. Don't allow me to get lost in television or video games for too long. I need to share my time with you and talk. Loss and grief are a time for sharing.

69. Please don't argue in front of me anymore. Parents should support and respect each other—regardless—in front of their children.

———————

70. It's not my job to make or change visitation plans.

71. Please don't be afraid of my
disliking you. That's all part of
my growing up. I need to be
allowed to have these feelings
sometimes.

———————

72. I will test you and try to get my
way, but remember I'm just a kid
who needs limits, no matter how
old I am.

73. Don't pass the buck to each other. Discipline me when it's necessary.

---

74. Please listen to me without judging me. These are hard times for me too.

---

75. Remind me to always clean up my own mess.

76. Please validate my feelings. They may be your feelings too. It will help both of us.

---

77. Please say "I'm sorry" when you make a mistake. It makes me feel better to know you are not perfect.

78. Please don't prolong good-byes when I have to leave. It makes me feel uncomfortable.

~~~~~~~~~~~~~~~

79. Actions speak louder than words. Please be careful.

80. I know you may not enjoy hearing your ex-spouse's voice on the other end of the telephone. A private phone number in my room will alleviate a lot of problems.

~~~~~~~~~~~~~~~~~~

81. I will need to have a curfew at both homes.

82. Please don't make me feel uncomfortable about your new relationships by asking me to keep secrets.

~~~~~~~~~~~~~~~

83. It may be painful for me to see you with another person in a loving relationship. Don't deny my feelings. Talk to me about it and help me to grow and accept new situations.

84. Don't force new relationships on me too soon. Be a good judge of timing.

~~~~~~~~~~~~~~

85. Complete honesty and integrity are necessary for the success of our new families.

~~~~~~~~~~~~~~

86. Please be courageous. Courage is the strength to do what is right regardless of the consequences.

87. My happiness depends on yours.
    Happiness is a state of well-being
    and contentment.

    ~~~~~~~~~~~~~~~~

88. Your enthusiasm will help me to
    embrace my new changes and
    life.

    ~~~~~~~~~~~~~~~~

89. Please model good behavior; I
    will copy it.

90. Please . . . no disclaimers. Don't say, "I'll let you, but I'm not going to like it."

————————

91. Don't threaten a punishment that you aren't going to follow through on.

————————

92. Please don't bargain with me. Tell me what you want and expect me to obey.

93. Please don't angrily tell me,
    "You're just like your (mother,
    father)."

    ~~~~~~~~~~~~

94. It is easier to reinforce good
    behavior than to punish bad
    behavior.

    ~~~~~~~~~~~~

95. Tell me stories about when you
    were a kid. This makes me feel
    closer to you.

96. Please keep photo albums of me around the house, so I can see how I am growing up.

~~~~~~~~~~~~~~~

97. Watch my favorite television show with me at your house.

~~~~~~~~~~~~~~~

98. Show me where you are when I'm not with you. Take me to work or your favorite place to eat.

99. Where a new relationship or stepparent is concerned, demand courtesy, but not love.

~~~~~~~~~~~~~~

100. Make sure I have time alone with my biological parent. If you are dating or remarried, please set aside special time for just the two of us.

101. Please communicate with my school regarding changes in family structure, routine, and relationships, so that they will be better aware of my needs, particularly during difficult times.

———————————

102. Please remind me as often as possible that it is not my fault you are divorcing. Tell me that divorce is a grown-up solution to a grown-up problem.

103. Tell me the truth. Divorce can be a very hard and painful thing for everyone.

----

104. If I catch you feeling sad or crying, please don't try to hide your feelings. But remember, it's scary for me to see my parent in pain too often or for too long.

105. Being on time is very important. Please pick me up and drop me off at agreed-upon times so no one, especially me, will have to worry.

~~~~~~~~~~~~~~~~

106. Please don't ask me everything that happened when I was with the other parent.

107. Please don't stand next to me or listen in when I am speaking to my other parent on the phone. This makes me feel uncomfortable and I may lose my trust in you if you become sneaky.

~~~~~~~~~~~~~~~~

108. Holidays are the hardest times for us. Please be sensitive during these special times.

109. Help me to clearly understand the rules in each house and be patient while I make mistakes.

---

110. There are two kinds of divorce Santas—present Santa and privilege Santa. Please try not to be either one. Don't let me get away with things I was never allowed to do. It's too confusing.

111. Don't try to please me by giving in to my sweet tooth or feeding me junk foods. I'll wind up getting sick and cranky and neither one of us will have any quality time.

~~~~~~~~~~~~~~~~

112. Presents won't make up for time. If you only give me presents and not time I'll know it's a cop-out on your part.

113. Please remember I don't want to take sides or get involved in your battles.

----

114. Sometimes I will try to manipulate you. Don't encourage or allow me to develop this trait.

115. Please don't try to hurt or control each other by using me as a tool or a weapon.

~~~~~~~~~~~~~~~~~

116. My opinions about your dating partners should not be solicited. I will tell you how I feel if and when I'm ready. This is your private adult business.

117. Please don't deny me my right to visit with both parents.

———————————

118. Remember that a child living with unhappily married parents more often gets into psychiatric difficulty than a child whose mismatched parents have been healthy and strong enough to sever their troubled relationship and have a healthy "divorced" relationship with their child.

119. Half-truths produce confusion and distrust. Truth, painful as it may be, brings trust and gives me the security of knowing exactly where I stand.

~~~~~~~~~~~~~~~~

120. Please set aside ten to fifteen minutes a day for us to be totally alone and together without interruption. This is a good time to share thoughts and feelings or feel safe and cozy.

121. Sometimes I may actually be happy you are divorced, because there is no more arguing in the house and I feel safe. Please don't be angry with me if I tell you I like your divorce.

122. Sometimes when I'm with Mom I may want to be with Dad and vice versa. This is a very confusing time. Please let me use the phone when I need to know you're still there.

---

123. I may cry more often or be more sensitive than usual. Please help me to feel safe again.

124. Remind me very often that you did not get a divorce because I was bad or did something wrong.

⌁⌁⌁⌁⌁⌁⌁⌁⌁⌁⌁⌁⌁⌁⌁

125. I may think it's your fault I'm sad or unhappy and blame you for my feelings. Please take the time to explain that the divorce was necessary for you and that you are sorry I have been hurt in making your adult decision.

126. Please don't blame each other for your divorce. It took two of you to decide to marry and two of you to make a situation that necessitated divorce.

------~~~~~~~~------

127. Please reassure me that my angry thoughts cannot harm anyone.

128. I may become overly worried
     and protective of you because
     there is only one of you in the
     house at a time. I may be afraid
     that one of you will die.
     Reassure me that there is always
     someone to love and take care
     of me.

     ~~~~~~~~~~~~~~~

129. Please don't cram a lot of fun
     activities into our visit, with
     little or no time to talk or
     cuddle.

130. Please don't tell me that you
don't like me to spend time
with my other parent.

- - - - - - - - - -

131. Please don't ever ask me to keep
secrets from my other parent.

132. Try to understand that sometimes I may not want to visit with you because I want to be with my friends for special occasions. I still love you. I'm just growing up.

———————

133. Please remember I need both of you to support and love me during times of crisis.

134. An unexpected hug or kiss will always make me feel terrific.

~~~~~~~~~~~~~~~

135. Please don't ask me to report on my other parent's new purchases and possessions.

~~~~~~~~~~~~~~~

136. Please try your best to keep me out of courtroom experiences.

137. Pets are part of our family. Please allow me to share them with both families.

~~~~~~~~~~~~~~~~

138. I really don't like having to pack things every weekend. Please try to help alleviate packing as much as possible.

139. Please don't ever forget that I can't thrive without lots of understanding and love.

~~~~~~~~~~~~~~

140. Don't be afraid to be firm with me. I am your child, not your buddy.

141. Please don't ask when you should be telling me what to do.

---

142. Set limits and teach me that there are consequences for my inappropriate actions.

---

143. Please don't ever embarrass me in front of others.

144. Please remember that the anger
I express toward a stepparent
might really be intended for the
biological parent, but the
stepparent is a safer target.

~~~~~~~~~~~~~~~~~~

145. Please allow me to adjust slowly
to step-siblings. Don't force us
to do everything together.

146. Please don't introduce me to all of your new dates. It's hard to picture you with anyone but my other parent.

~~~~~~~~~~~~~~~~~~

147. Use discretion about your intimate relationships. Off weekends are perfect for your intimate experiences with others.

148. I do not want to discuss my other parent's dating habits or friends with you. Please don't question me and try to pry into affairs that are not yours.

~~~~~~~~~~~~~~~

149. Don't split up brothers and sisters. We need each other.

150. Please don't let the divorce stop us from having fun. I'm still a kid.

~~~~~~~~~~~~~~~~~

151. Sometimes I have scary dreams. Listen carefully and try to help me feel safe.

152. Please tell me ahead of time when, where, and with whom I am spending holidays and vacations.

~~~~~~~~~~~~~~~~~~~

153. Please allow me to have my own names for people. I may want to leave out the word "step" for mom, dad, brother, or sister.

154. Please remember how confusing it can be when we live in the same house and have different last names.

~~~~~~~~~~~~~~~

155. Please know that sometimes when I say I want to be alone, I may really need people to help or hug me.

156. Sometimes I feel like I have to be older and more grown up to help take care of you. Please remind me that I am the child and you are the parent. I really don't want so much responsibility.

~~~~~~~~~~~~~~

157. I like visiting you, but please take into consideration what activities will be fun for both of us and be flexible.

158. A large family still requires individual time for each child. Try to make us all feel special and cared for.

~~~~~~~~~~~~~~~~~

159. A list of activities for the future is always a wonderful idea for everyone to look forward to.

160. Please be careful how and why you talk about my mom or dad to me.

----

161. Please keep a calendar in the house just for us. It really hurts when you forget birthdays, recitals, music lessons, sports practices, or games.

162. Please remember I should always have a way to contact an absent parent in case of emergency.

~~~~~~~~~~~~~~~~

163. Please don't withdraw your love from me when I misbehave.

164. I know you are sometimes upset. Please don't let your emotional state determine your discipline.

————————————

165. Please teach me responsibility by sometimes letting me experience the consequences of my actions, as long as they are not life threatening.

166. Please be generous with your touches and hugs. I can feel very lonely during a divorce or separation.

---

167. Please tell me how much you like me and how happy you are to spend time with me. It will help me to feel more secure.

168. Try to create some family traditions in both homes, even if it's having pizza every Friday night. It makes me feel safe.

~~~~~~~~~~~~~~~

169. Help me to become self-sufficient. It is a positive part of my growth.

170. Teach and encourage me to set goals for myself.

~~~~~~~~~~~~~~~

171. Please tell Grandma and Grandpa that I may need extra love during this time in my life and not criticism of the other parent.

172. Please try to have curb pickup and drop-off or school pickup and drop-off if you're not able to control negative confrontations in front of me.

----

173. Please pay close attention to my schoolwork. If I begin to perform poorly, help me. The divorce can upset me more than you are aware of.

174. Talk to my teachers during times of stress and change and have them watch my actions and reactions to social situations with my peers.

―――――――――

175. Pay close attention to the frequency of illnesses I may have during the divorce or separation. My mind can really overwork and overstress my body.

176. Don't grill me about things that are private to Mom or Dad. It makes me feel like a traitor either way I react.

———————————

177. I might need someone else to talk with besides my parents. Please encourage me and give me permission and help to do so.

178. Yes, I may look or act like the other parent, but it's not my fault. Please continue to love and accept me or get help if you have a difficult time dealing with the similarities.

~~~~~~~~~~~~

179. Only you can validate my worth by letting me know that you are happy I am your child. Show and tell me this often.

180. Little notes of encouragement, happy faces, stickers, stars, CDs, favorite magazines, or books can really brighten my day. Please try to remember that.

----

181. You both chose to bring me into this world. Please love, protect, and nurture my mind, heart, and body.

182. You may feel disappointed in your failed marriage, but please continue to celebrate your successful creation—*me!*